My F Words

Consultants

Ashley Bishop, Ed.D.
Sue Bishop, M.E.D.

Publishing Credits

Dona Herweck Rice, *Editor-in-Chief*

Robin Erickson, *Production Director*

Lee Aucoin, *Creative Director*

Sharon Coan, *Project Manager*

Jamey Acosta, *Editor*

Rachelle Cracchiolo, M.A.Ed., *Publisher*

Image Credits

cover Radius Images/Getty Images; p.2 Kletr/Shutterstock; p.3 Radius Images/Getty Images; p.4 MarFot/Shutterstock; p.5 Alexander Raths/Shutterstock; p.6 sbarabu/Shutterstock; p.7 karin claus/Shutterstock; p.8 R. Gino Santa Maria/Shutterstock; p.9 3445128471/Shutterstock; p.10 Ultrashock/Shutterstock; back cover Kletr/Shutterstock

Teacher Created Materials

5301 Oceanus Drive
Huntington Beach, CA 92649-1030
http://www.tcmpub.com

ISBN 978-1-4333-2549-6

© 2012 Teacher Created Materials, Inc.
Printed in Malaysia
THU001.50393

I see a **f**ish.

see a **f**irefighter.

I see a **f**ork.

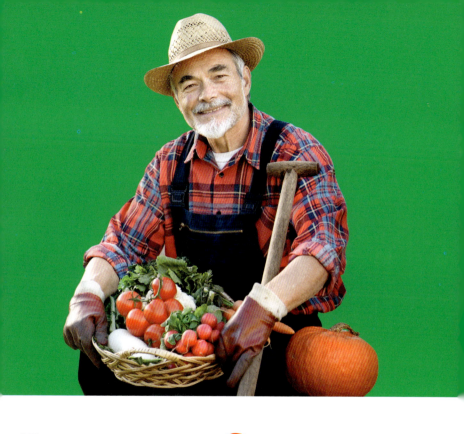

I see a farmer.

I see a **f**ire.

I see a **f**eather.

I see a face.

I see a **fox**.

Glossary

Sight Words

I   see   a

Activities

- Read the book aloud to your child, pointing to the *f* words as you read them. After reading each page, ask, "What do you see?"

- Discuss with your child the importance of firefighters and what they do for the community. Tell your child that firefighters put out fires. Remind him or her that the word *firefighter* begins with *f*.

- If your child eats fish, cook fish for dinner and talk about how you need to eat it with a fork. Ask your child what other foods he or she eats with a fork that starts with the letter *f*. Remind him or her that the word *fish* and *fork* begins with *f*.

- Have your child draw or paint a portrait of his or her face. Discuss the different parts of a face and what they do.

- Help your child think of a personally valuable word to represent the letter *f*, such as *father* or *friend*.